How to be Happy

Paul Nicholson SJ

All booklets are published
thanks to the generosity of the supporters
of the Catholic Truth Society

All rights reserved. First published 2019 by The Incorporated Catholic Truth Society, 42-46 Harleyford Road London SE11 5AY. Tel: 020 7640 0042 / Fax: 020 7640 0046 www.ctsbooks.org. Copyright © 2019 The Incorporated Catholic Truth Society.

ISBN 978 1 78469 604 7

Contents

1. The Pursuit of Happiness 5
   - Elusive happiness 5
   - To look redeemed 7

2. Four False Trails to Happiness 11
   - Made happy by what I have 13
   - Striving for perfection 14
   - Work harder and longer 17
   - Comfort, without challenge 18

3. Help Yourself to Happiness 21
   - Mind, Body, Spirit 22
   - Self-help 24
   - Stoicism and detachment 25
   - Fulfilment 27

4. Four Pillars of Happiness 31
   - Relationships 32
   - Morality and conscience 33
   - Gratitude 35
   - The examined life 38

5. Happiness as Personal 41
   - What makes you happy? 42
   - "Know thyself" 43

6. Practices Promoting Happiness 47
    Focus elsewhere 48
    Monitoring 49
    Service 52
    Sense of purpose 54

7. Happiness as Gift 57
    Happiness as gift, not achievement 57
    An afterword on heaven 59

1. The Pursuit of Happiness

Let no one ever come to you without leaving better and happier. Be the living expression of God's kindness: kindness in your face, kindness in your eyes, kindness in your smile.

Mother Teresa

Elusive happiness

Do you want to be happy? Really? There are from the outset at least two good reasons for thinking that the answer to that question is "Yes". The first is the very fact that you have picked out, and are now reading, a booklet called *How to be Happy*. But the second is more general. It seems almost self-evident that happiness is something that everyone wants, most of the time. Indeed, one way of describing the kind of motivation that underlies almost everything that we do as human beings, throughout the whole of our lives, is to think of it as the pursuit of happiness.

It is, though, truly a pursuit. Few people would claim that they are happy all the time, and many spend a long time looking for happiness without seeming to find it.

Even during those minutes, or weeks, or years, when you are happy, you can at the very same time be aware that this is a state that is unlikely to be permanent. Of course, you can try very hard to hold on to whatever seemed to make you happy in the first place. Experience suggests, though, that it doesn't often work, and that happiness fades when clung to too tightly. You can perhaps try to get around this by storing up happy memories, but those memories themselves can be painful when recalled in later, less happy times.

Still, happiness certainly remains worth pursuing. Before you read any further, pause and take a moment now to remember a time when you were happy. And do this in such a way not just to remember it, but to try to relive it. Maybe it was the first time that you were in love, or got to hold your new-born child or grandchild; you might recall the best holiday that you ever had, or a book or film that you really enjoyed. You might have been happy walking by yourself in a quiet place, or dancing until dawn in a crowded party. Wherever you were, whoever you were with, and whatever you were doing, see if you can get back in touch here and now with what you were feeling then, how it was to be happy there, in that particular time and space.

If you succeeded in that little exercise and were able to experience again something, at least, of how you feel when you're happy, then the chances are that you would want to feel like that again. And that's why the title of this booklet, *How to be Happy* is important. Because happiness isn't something like good weather, that we have no control over, and just have to wait until it arrives (and enjoy it when it does!) Happiness is something that we can to some extent at least work towards, or open ourselves up to – there are things that we can do to help ourselves be happy. Looking at what some of these things are, and how they work, is one of the main aims of these pages.

To look redeemed

Of course, everything that has been said so far runs the risk of looking like selfishness, more or less thinly disguised. Certainly Christian faith has often been preached in such a way that it appeared to concentrate more on virtues like self-giving and sacrificial service than on promoting the search for, or the pursuit of, happiness. Yet there are good reasons for thinking that, even from a more narrowly focussed faith perspective, happiness is something that is worth working at.

In the nineteenth century the German philosopher Friedrich Nietzsche proclaimed the death of God. One of the reasons for his atheism was that he considered that Christians used God as a shelter or escape from the real world, something that stopped them from being self-reliant in the ways that he thought important for all human beings. But he also said, on one occasion, that what stopped him from being a Christian was that the Christians whom he encountered didn't look redeemed.

Here they were, proclaiming what was potentially some of the best news the world had ever heard: that they, and indeed all human beings, had been rescued from everything that threatened human life, and even from death itself, by an all-powerful and loving God. And yet, for all that, in Nietzsche's experience, they went around looking every bit as miserable and worn down by the cares of life as everybody else!

The truth is that people find themselves drawn to others who look happy, and even more to those who are in reality enjoying that state. When we see someone like that, we want to know their secret. Because there is much about human life that is challenging, and tiring, and can easily wear people down, and happy people are no more exempt from those aspects of the human condition than anybody else. So perhaps, in coming close to people like that, who seem to have the knack of being happy despite suffering from the same trials as everybody else, it is possible to learn from them, and thus become happier in our own lives.

Seen in this light, being happy, and even looking happy, can actually be seen as part of Christian witness, a way of drawing others to faith. For what Nietzsche intuited is certainly true. Christians do have a supreme reason for recognising that the hardships of daily living are outweighed by something more important and more fundamental. That "something" is indeed the news that we have been redeemed, that God in Christ has promised to stand alongside us at all times, and ultimately to bring us to be with him in happiness forever.

So if I can be happy, and look happy, I am more likely to be able to help other people who are trying to do the same. My happiness itself gives me a chance to witness to its source, which, as we shall explore in these pages, is ultimately the gift of God. So it is not always selfish to want to be happy. It may, indeed, be the best possible service that I can offer to the people round about me.

Considering those other people points to a limitation of this present work. Although it will analyse happiness in the context of people who live in contact with others, interacting with them on a daily basis, its main focus is personal happiness. In other words, other people are thought of principally in terms of how they can contribute to the happiness of an individual, or at best of how some kinds of interactions with others (for instance, being of service to them) will in fact make it more likely that the said individual will become a happier person. A fuller coverage of happiness from a Christian perspective would look more closely at the happiness of the community, not simply the individual, and all the factors that make for that. Indeed, it would be possible to argue that, as a follower of Christ, I can only truly be happy as part of a community that is itself content, or at least as one of a group of individuals living together in such a way as to have that mutual happiness as one of their aims.

2. Four False Trails to Happiness

To say that somebody is happy can have so many different meanings: they're in love, they're drunk, they're high, they're enjoying themselves, they're exultant, they're content, they're jovial, they're lucky, they're in high spirits, they have found the perfect life.

Abbot Christopher Jamison OSB, Finding Happiness

Do you know the difference between a maze and a labyrinth? There is a famous maze at Hampton Court outside London, a series of dense hedges planted in such a way as to leave a narrow twisting path between them. As people walk along this path, they encounter many dead-ends, forcing them to go back and select another choice at points where the path forks. Unless you know the maze well, it is almost impossible to reach the centre, the goal of the journey, without encountering a number of these blocked routes and going back to try again.

One of the best-known labyrinths is set into the floor of Chartres Cathedral in France. It is thought to date back to the thirteenth century. Although the trail here is marked out by stone slabs set into the cathedral floor, rather than by high hedges, at first sight the experience of entering into the Chartres labyrinth's journey seems rather similar to that of venturing into the Hampton Court maze. But there is a key difference; Chartres has no dead-ends. It is true that its path twists back and forth, at times coming close to the centre, only to veer away again; but anyone who walks its route steadily will inevitably come to the centre, and then be led just as surely back to the periphery, and to life beyond the labyrinth's borders. The owners of Hampton Court feel the need to employ a warder on a high platform, available to guide those who are lost in the maze back to its entrance. In a labyrinth you cannot get lost in this way.

So is the path to true happiness more like a maze or a labyrinth? Is there a single path that, providing you start at the right place and don't stray, will inevitably bring people to the bliss that is their goal? Or will a journey to happiness almost inevitably involve taking some wrong turns, and having to go back, and try again, perhaps repeatedly, before the goal is reached? Experience suggests that the second of these is closer to the truth: the path to happiness is like a maze. The good news, though, is that a lot can be learnt from the dead-ends and false trails, and so the next steps on the journey here will involve looking at four of the most common of these, and see what they can add to an understanding of what it is to be happy, and how to reach that state.

Made happy by what I have

One of the most widespread images in our society today of what would make a person happy is that of a huge lottery win. There can be few people who haven't dreamed, at one time or another, whether they play the lottery or not, of what they would do if they were suddenly, and unexpectedly, to come into a fortune. Never having to work again, the big car, the new house, the swimming pool and the exotic holiday. It's a pleasant day-dream to pass an empty half-hour, but most of the time it is then simply dismissed. For one thing, the odds against coming into a fortune in this way make it very unlikely. Beyond that, though, there is also the sneaking suspicion that having any, or even all, of these things still wouldn't guarantee happiness.

In 1961 a Yorkshire woman, Viv Nicholson, won more than £150,000 on the football pools, a sum equivalent to maybe four million pounds today. Asked by a new reporter what she was going to do with the money, she replied that she was going to "Spend, spend, spend." And that is what she and her husband (who at the time of the win was in a job that paid £7 per week) did. Over the next four years they spent the entire amount on all the things that consumerism suggests lead to happiness. But when her husband died in a car crash in 1965, she was already left with huge debts. Her story caught, and stays in, the popular imagination, being portrayed in a television play in 1977 and a musical in 1999. She herself suggested that it was only when she became a Jehovah's Witness later in life that she found something of the happiness that had eluded her in her years of fabulous wealth.

It would be wrong, of course, to draw conclusions that are too simple from Viv Nicholson's story, concluding, for instance, that money can never bring happiness. Hers was a complex situation. Clearly ill-prepared for a change in her circumstances of this magnitude, the pools win had the effect of cutting her off from her roots and all that had until then supported her. It is also clear that for some of the time after the win she did enjoy some happiness. But her history does illustrate something that deep-down we know to be true. The promise made by consumerism, that we can be made happy simply by what we have, and made happier by having more, is simply false. To pursue happiness by striving to have more things is, ultimately, to go down a dead-end in the maze.

Striving for perfection

If what a person has cannot be guaranteed to make them happy, perhaps a better path would be to concentrate on what a person is. After all, Jesus said, according to the gospel of Matthew, "Be perfect, just as your heavenly Father is perfect" (*Mt* 5:48). Perhaps I will discover the route to happiness by striving to become the best person that it is possible for me to be.

This sounds initially a little more promising than a plan simply to amass possessions. As a strategy, however, it is clearly incomplete. After all, the idea of becoming "the best person possible" doesn't answer the question of what kind of person that is. For one it might be a question of physical fitness, regular training to bring my body to the peak of its powers; for another, it can be a moral perfection that is being sought, that a person strives to be good in all circumstances, even (or perhaps especially) when this is costly. Or maybe it is a matter of being surrounded by the right people, keeping in with the right crowd, and being seen in all the right places.

The more you try to pin down the kind of perfection that is being looked for, the less likely it seems to guarantee happiness. Certainly, if happiness is only to be gained once the goal of perfection, or whatever kind, is reached, then this path almost certainly leads to a dead-end. A torn hamstring, a debilitating illness, or eventually simply old age, are enough to knock a quest for physical perfection off track. Those who aim at moral perfection sooner or later share the experience of St Paul, who in writing to the Christian community in Rome reflected ruefully, "For I have the desire to do what is good, but I cannot carry it out. For I do not do the good I want to do, but the evil I do not want to do – this I keep on doing." (*Rm* 7: 18-19). And trying to constantly surround yourself with the right crowd is notoriously unreliable, as they drift off to other venues or a new generation takes their place.

If, then, the achieving of perfection in any of its chosen forms is not to be guaranteed, and indeed in many circumstances is inherently unlikely, this would seem to be one more dead-end. Could it be though that happiness is not to be found in the achievement of, but in the striving for, perfection in these ways? Perhaps those who dedicate their lives to the attempt to find perfection are made happy simply by that attempt itself. The musical *Man of La Mancha*, based on the story of Don Quixote, tells the story of a Spanish gentleman who dedicates himself single-handedly to reviving knight-errantry. A key moment in the play comes when he sings a song entitled "To Dream the Impossible Dream". Quixote, at least in that moment of relative lucidity (for much of the story he simply seems to be deluded), recognises that the dream he has will not, and indeed cannot, ever be achieved. Yet for him at this juncture perhaps the quest itself will prove to be enough, and will lead him, almost incidentally, to discover happiness along the way.

There is something in this belief, and we will return to it later as we try to assemble the elements of a happy life. But to concentrate too hard on the striving at the expense of the goal can itself lead to another wrong turn in the maze, a wrong turn that is a particularly common trap in the present day.

Work harder and longer

In Lewis Carroll's book *Through the Looking Glass* the White Queen offers Alice (of *Alice in Wonderland* fame) employment in her service. One of the perks of the job, she is told, is "jam every other day". This is then explained as meaning "jam tomorrow and jam yesterday – but never jam today". Alice can work as hard as she is able, but will never reach the day when she receives this reward. Unsurprisingly, she turns down the job offer.

Alice sees through the deceitful promise in a way that is not always easy for our contemporaries in Western society. Though some years ago the advent of mechanisation and labour-saving devices seemed to be pointing to a future of less work and more leisure, with the implication that this would lead people to greater happiness, in fact the opposite has happened. Employment in many parts of the world actually seems less secure than it was a few decades ago. People have to work for longer hours, have less leisure, and enjoy fewer rights to holidays, pensions, and other "bonuses", than used to be the case. So in an attempt to reach the things that they presume will make for happiness, they work harder, get more stressed, and frequently experience the work environment as a seemingly endless treadmill. "Jam tomorrow" indeed!

It is worth admitting that there is no obvious and quick way out of this situation. Just employment practices, adequate living standards for all, and the removal of glaring global inequalities have never, and will never, be achieved without long, painstaking, collective effort. But a first step here might be to recognise more clearly the falsity of the implicit promise in this kind of consumerism: that if only people put more effort in, work harder, and accept that everything else in life must be subservient to this work ethic they will (eventually) be happy. This is a false promise, and this path to happiness is another wrong turning.

Comfort, without challenge

Once you have seen through the promise of "jam tomorrow" for the deceit that it is, it can be tempting to move to the other end of the spectrum in a quest for happiness. This might be summed up as "anything for a quiet life". Maybe the goal should be simply to live as quietly and comfortably as you can, avoiding challenging situations and difficult people whenever possible. No doubt this approach will call for a degree of realism; none of these challenges is likely to be wholly avoidable, at least over the course of a lifetime, but for someone who doesn't set their hopes too high or expect too much, a quiet withdrawn life may bring a sufficient measure of happiness.

Of all the blind alleys explored so far, in many ways at first glance this may seem to have the most to commend it. Indeed there are reputable philosophical positions, as we shall see later on, that have this kind of starting point. But instinctively, I imagine, to many readers of this booklet, this route to happiness will appear to be something of a surrender. After all, its logical end-point is that "rest in peace" that we associate with those who have recently died. To that extent it seems like an escape from the world and all that it offers. Perhaps there are a few hermits who have set out along this route in the hope of finding happiness, although many hermits are themselves, in my experience, very much involved in the world and its struggles as they hold these before God in prayer.

Even if this could be shown to be a successful path to happiness, it is not one that is open to many. Most people, by the time that they become adults, are caught up in a whole web of commitments: to family, friends, colleagues, work and leisure pursuits and others. Freeing yourself from all of these is not a realistic option, nor is it one that is likely to appear attractive. Happiness is not to be found for most of us in a wholly comfortable life lived without challenge.

So far the effort here has been to clear the ground, to recognise paths to happiness that appear to offer a certain degree of plausibility, but that are ultimately dead-ends, offering unproductive false promises. Happiness is not to be found by amassing more and more material goods. It cannot rely on my ability to attain perfection, in myself or those around me. The ever-faster treadmill of a working life gives no guarantee of happiness now or in the future, and to rely on being able to live a quiet and unchallenged life of comfort is for most of us a goal that is impossible, unattractive, and ultimately fruitless. It is time, then, to turn to the more positive aspects of this journey.

3. Help Yourself to Happiness

We cannot be happy if we expect to live all the time at the highest peak of intensity. Happiness is not a matter of intensity but of balance and order and rhythm and harmony.

Thomas Merton, No Man is an Island

Maybe at this point it is worth changing from the image of the maze to that of the labyrinth. With some, at least, of the main dead-ends and blind alleys on the journey to happiness marked out in the hope that they can be avoided, some of the stepping-stones that lead towards that central goal can be looked at more closely. A number of these will be shared with people coming from very different world-views and faith perspectives. Others will be given a particular slant when viewed through a Christian lens. Others again may prove to be comprehensible only by those who share a common faith.

This third chapter of *How to be Happy* looks particularly at what might be learnt from the kind of writing on the topic that can be found in the self-help manuals that are a common feature of bookshops today. Why is it that they have become so popular, and what might be taken from them to try and build up a more comprehensive picture of the topic being considered here?

Mind, Body, Spirit

When the Catholic Truth Society talked about commissioning this booklet, two considerations came to the fore. The first was very positive: books on happiness, and how to achieve it, are popular. They are clearly meeting a need felt by many people today. Some of these people are themselves, no doubt, unhappy, and are looking for ways to escape from this unpleasant situation. Many others, though, may well be perfectly content in a day-to-day sort of way, but would like to be happier, or are interested in seeing how other people go about the quest for happiness. The other consideration was more challenging: because these books are popular, there are huge numbers of different titles available already. How can this one stand out, what is going to be distinctive about it? Some of the response to that last question may be becoming clear already, and it will continue to be addressed in the pages ahead. In answering it, though, it is worth thinking about where books on happiness are to be found.

Some years ago, general bookshops might have had a section, consisting of at least a few shelves, devoted to religious books. In those days these would almost all have been written from a Christian perspective. There might have been bibles, prayer books, and perhaps a few spiritual classics by writers such as Teresa of Avila or Thomas Merton. Nowadays religious books are more likely to be discovered not in their own little enclave, but in a larger section with a title like "Mind, Body, Spirit". Christian books will sit alongside those drawing on Islam, Judaism, Hinduism and other faiths. Mindfulness approaches rooted in Buddhism seem particularly popular at the moment. There may well be self-help books, and those presenting different philosophical understandings of how to live a good and fulfilled life. This change in, and indeed expansion of, what might be broadly considered to be "religious" publishing is perhaps surprising, at a time when it had seemed until recently that religious faith was losing out to more secular understandings of the world.

One way of thinking about what is going on here, a way that fits well with our topic of the search for happiness, is to think of the heading that groups these different books together: "Mind, Body, Spirit". If specifically religious books were, and maybe still are, expected to be concerned mainly with the spirit, now there is more of a desire to place specifically spiritual questions firmly in the context of the mind and body as well, to adopt, what is called a more "holistic" approach, as popular jargon would have it.

Christians should welcome this change of emphasis. Ours is not, and has never been, a purely spiritual outlook on questions of faith. We believe, after all, in a God who became human, a Word that became flesh, Jesus as the incarnate Son of God. The Christian journey to God is one that includes mind, body and spirit, and any Christian understanding of happiness will also need to pay attention to each of these, and to the various ways in which they relate to one another.

Self-help

There is another feature that unites many of the large number of books about happiness that are currently available; they are written in a way that is often described as "self-help". These are above all practical works. They are not primarily concerned with the theory of happiness, analysing terms or tracing the historical development of concepts. Nor are they purely descriptive, presenting different ways in which various people and cultures understand what it is to be happy, where they agree and where they differ. Instead, the promise of these works, and no doubt the reason that they have become so popular, is that if you read them and follow what they say, you too will become as happy as, it may be presumed, the book's author.

Of course, not all of these books are of the same value. As we have already seen, there are many blind alleys on the path to happiness. But the idea that we can indeed help ourselves, at least to some extent, to be happier is an important one. In many aspects of life, individual and social, it is one thing to simply understand or interpret a situation; it can, though, be more useful to work to change it. This outlook resonates deeply with many people today. If I am unhappy, I am less interested in merely understanding my unhappiness or its opposite. What I want is to be able to change the situation that I find myself in, and if possible find a guide who will show me how to do this, preferably sooner rather than later.

Clearly this distinction between understanding and changing a situation can be pushed too far. Often the best way to start changing something (or indeed someone) is to understand it better. And similarly, in working to bring about change, it is possible to come to a clearer understanding of that which is being worked on. But any consideration of how to be happy would do well to bear in mind that much of this is concerned with a set of practical skills, skills that can be learnt and passed on to others. Self-help is a predominantly practical outlook on life, and one that is as relevant to a Christian understanding of the world and the people in it as it is to the perspective coming from any other faith-view or none.

Stoicism and detachment

An earlier section here concluded that hoping to find happiness by looking for an entirely comfortable life, found by avoiding challenges wherever possible, was one of the blind alleys that are best avoided. But there is another, related, outlook, which shares something in common with this, yet does offer a more helpful contribution to our search.

Stoicism is a philosophy developed in ancient Greece which holds that human beings can and should accept whatever they encounter in the present moment, while cultivating an attitude that enables them to escape from the desire for pleasure or happiness, and indeed from the fear of pain. Unlike the idea of happiness of comfort rejected above, stoics do not necessarily try and avoid situations of challenge or conflict. They rather train themselves to be relatively unaffected by them, by concentrating instead on living virtuous lives. Only in this way, they believe, can happiness be found.

This approach has something in common with the Buddhist teaching that suffering is ultimately a result of a failure to understand the world, and our place within it, correctly. One way of conceiving Buddhism is as a series of practices which will enable the practitioner to escape this illusory understanding, and thus come to a place where suffering is no more. Although doing this will not necessarily bring about happiness – it could be argued that the idea of happiness as it is being used here is every bit as illusory as suffering – it emphasises the fact that there are things that can be done to eliminate unhappiness, that by training our minds we can affect the way that we view the world, and alter our responses to it.

In fact these approaches find echoes in a traditional Christian concept, itself much influenced by Greek stoic thought, that of detachment. This suggests that it is possible to enjoy all the good things in God's creation, including those who surrounded us, without becoming wholly caught up in them. It goes further and says that moreover this is in fact the only way to be truly happy. Without detachment there is the risk of being enslaved by these good things, becoming dependent upon them in ways that can be devastating when they are no longer present. Such enslavement is unlikely to be clear to a person until they have travelled far along its road. But by schooling myself in detachment I am able both to enjoy such good things as come my way, and be relatively unaffected when they are no longer available to me.

Fulfilment

One other idea that features largely in any contemporary discussion of happiness is that of fulfilment. The desire for fulfilment can be a powerful impetus to change. The archetypal mid-life crisis pictures a person throwing over commitments and relationships that may have shaped their lives for decades in the hope of finding greater fulfilment elsewhere – with a younger partner, a different job, a faster car. In this understanding, a fulfilled person is a happy person, and at its extremes no one and nothing should be allowed to come in the way of pursuing that fulfilment.

There are, it is obvious, risks to adopting this outlook. The most obvious is that it offers no guarantees. The fact that someone does not feel fulfilled where they are does not make it certain that they will automatically be better off by moving elsewhere, no matter how radical the move. The proverb that states that "the grass is always greener on the other side of the fence" encapsulates hard-won wisdom. At the very least caution should be urged upon anyone wanting to make major changes in their life in the hope of becoming a more fulfilled person.

Another thing to notice is that the idea of fulfilment has no more content that that of happiness itself. One person may consider that a life dedicated to the service of others will bring them fulfilment. Another may argue that only a capacity for untrammelled self-expression will be enough to achieve this. In linking happiness and fulfilment we risk using one ambiguous idea to explain another, and it is far from clear that doing so takes us any further forward in knowing how to be happy.

What the idea of fulfilment does usefully bring to centre-stage however is a reminder that happiness is above all something interior, which can be enjoyed across a wide range of exterior situations. If happiness is dependent upon possessing all, and more, than I need, or being surrounded by all, and only, those people whom I find most conducive, then a figure like Mother Teresa, devoting herself to tending the poorest of the poor in the back streets of Calcutta, is unlikely to ever be happy. But even those who couldn't dream of working in this way themselves are able to recognise that she found fulfilment in living as she did, and with it a deep happiness that proved infectious for many of those with whom she came into contact. Even a hard-bitten journalist like Malcom Muggeridge, who thought of himself as one of "the walking-wounded from the ideological conflicts of the age", could be won over by the love that radiated from her.

4. Four Pillars of Happiness

Sin is ultimately a refusal to believe that what God wants is my happiness and fulfilment.

Attributed to St Ignatius of Loyola

In this chapter we move from ideas that can help us think about happiness more clearly to some of its essential elements. There can be, I want to suggest, no real concept of happiness, at least one coming from a Christian perspective, that doesn't involve the four elements discussed below: relationships, morality, gratitude and the examined life. Insofar as one or other of these is absent, a person cannot be truly happy. That is not to say, however, that the four cannot take very different forms in different lives. Nor does what is written here mean to imply that these four alone are enough to guarantee happiness. So the title of the chapter refers to "four pillars", rather than "the four pillars". You may yourself be able to identify other elements that you consider essential for your own happiness, or indeed happiness in general.

Relationships

"It is not good for the human being to be alone". These are God's words, as reported in the first chapter of Genesis. And indeed, for most of us, it is impossible to imagine being truly happy if stranded alone on a desert island for any length of time. Precisely how other human beings contribute to an individual's happiness may vary greatly between different people. For an extravert, relaxation comes from being surrounded by, and interacting with, others. Introverts seek more time to themselves to process and benefit from what has gone on in their dealings with those around them. But introverts and extraverts alike are profoundly affected by the views and outlooks of other people, by their relationships with them and by learning to see the world through their eyes.

It is not just any kind of relationship that will make for happiness, of course. Abusive relationships, those where one person attempts to control or exploit another, where they are in it only for what they can gain themselves and offer little in return – all of these are more likely to provoke unhappiness than its contrary. Yet the power of relationship is such that at times people will settle even for these kinds of deceptive bonds, rather than being left without anyone to whom they can relate. The growing awareness of the suffering caused by loneliness often – though by no means exclusively – in the elderly, likewise points to the importance of relationships for a happy life.

In general it can be said that it is loving relationships that contribute most to happiness. That is not to say that other relationships are insignificant from this perspective. To operate as part of a well-motivated team, where everyone knows their role and feels able to contribute from their own skills and talents, may well make for a happy work environment. But love would most often seem to be a key element here. In his book, *The Four Loves*, C.S. Lewis distinguishes between four kinds of love, each of which is capable of contributing to the kind of relationship that leads to happiness. Three are naturally characteristic of human beings: empathy, friendship, and erotic attraction. The fourth, and greatest, is that unconditional love to be found in God which can also be, in Lewis's view, cultivated as a specifically Christian virtue. While the first three can contain, and indeed cloak, elements of selfishness, the fourth is wholly dedicated to the well-being of the other, and so will lay the foundation for the fullest, most genuine happiness.

Morality and conscience

It is a common human experience that bad people often seem to thrive while good people suffer, and indeed that the thriving of the bad may be a direct consequence of, and dependent upon, the suffering of the good. Many of the Hebrew psalms worry away at this experience, wondering why God allows it and challenging him about it. One theory as to how the concept of an afterlife gradually took root among the Jews is precisely because it was needed to redress the balance, to provide a forum in which justice, at the Last Judgement if not before, would finally be seen to be done.

Despite all this experience which appears initially at least to suggest otherwise, it would seem to be a deep-rooted human instinct that to be truly happy it is necessary to lead, or at least to attempt to lead, a morally good life. Certainly it must be difficult to be happy if you have a conscience that is constantly chiding you, and while human ingenuity has discovered many ways of silencing even the most insistent voice of conscience, that voice will often find other ways through which to make itself heard. It is probably not possible, this side of the grave at least, to prove that ultimately moral living and happiness are inseparable. But any understanding that looks to a Christian foundation is likely to want to take that understanding as a basic premise.

Nor is this instinct wholly reliant on Christian faith. Films, plays and novels with no specific Christian foundation have plots in which the villain is eventually brought to justice, and meets his or her come-uppance. Shakespeare's *Macbeth* is simply one example among very many. Indeed, such a narrative is often imposed on historical events. Much of the Hebrew Bible was edited by those who credited the times of Israel's flourishing to the leadership of good and moral leaders, and its falling into the hands of its enemies to periods when evil kings occupied the throne. In our own times, wars are frequently justified by the need to overthrow evil rulers whose continued grip on power prevents the well-being and happiness of their subjects.

Going deeper here is complicated by the fact of the near-impossibility of living a fully moral life. Christians believe that Jesus himself was able to do this, and many share the view that his mother Mary was similarly blessed. But the rest of us are all more or less sinful people, never wholly docile to the promptings of conscience. It becomes difficult, then, to ascribe all happiness to moral virtue, or all unhappiness to transgression. The parable of the wheat and weeds told in Chapter 13 of St Matthew's gospel well describes the situation that we are all likely to find ourselves in throughout our lives on this earth. From this viewpoint it takes, perhaps, an act of faith to affirm that morality and happiness belong together. It is, though, an act of faith firm enough to serve as a pillar of the outlook presented here.

Gratitude

One of the basic foundations of any life shaped by religious faith is the acknowledgement that every good thing that we enjoy is ultimately a gift. We did not create ourselves, bring ourselves into being; nor did we create everything around us that we rely on. We need other people to provide for us, and in the end we can only rely upon God to raise us from death. As soon as you begin to see the world in this light, it becomes clear that the only appropriate response is gratitude. Gratitude to God, in the first instance, and gratitude to the people around me. And so that gratitude becomes one of the pillars that is essential for the life of anyone who strives to be happy.

In the *Spiritual Exercises* of St Ignatius Loyola, his programme for deepening a relationship with God, and coming to a greater clarity about what God's call looks like in the life of any individual, Ignatius makes much of gratitude. It appears first as a response to the awareness of myself as created by God in order to love and serve him. As I come to know the reality of my own sinfulness more fully, gratitude is the response to God's constant, faithful and loving forgiveness. In prayerfully pondering the life of Christ, I see with greater clarity the practical steps that I can take in order to walk alongside him, and find myself grateful to be so called. And after contemplatively accompanying Jesus through his death and resurrection, I am invited to go back out into the world with the expectation of meeting God in all things and all people, and so continuing the cycle of thanksgiving.

The happiness that is the fruit of this gratitude takes on a particular shape for Ignatius, one that he calls consolation. It is a kind of joy, although one that is not necessarily accompanied by party balloons and alleluias (though it may be!) Rather, it is rooted in an awareness of living the kind of life that God has created me for. This is not some kind of static blueprint, but an invitation to use all the creativity with which I have been blessed to consider what I have to do in the most loving, Christ-like way in any situation.

Consolation can take a variety of different forms, not all of which are obviously connected with happiness, but one of them is the feeling of being in the right place at the right time, doing the right thing. You apply for a new job, maybe with some trepidation about making such a career move. Six months later, it is all working out really well. You find yourself as part of a good team, doing satisfying work, that stretches you but without undue stress. Here happiness and spiritual consolation are closely linked.

Perhaps, though, on another occasion, consolation takes on another shape. Through prayer you come to a deeper awareness of how you have hurt someone close to you. Perhaps you'd been trying to ignore this. Now, though, you find that you cannot ignore the issue any longer. As you see more clearly the harm that you've done, you feel bad. This is not an obvious happiness. But if the experience leads you to resolve to put things right, even if this can only be done at some cost to yourself, then it will be experienced as consolation. You are discovering yourself blessed with the power to become a more loving, Christ-like person. There is a happiness in that which can co-exist with the pain of knowing your own past failure, and the challenge of doing what you can to put it right.

The examined life

The Greek philosopher Plato recorded much of the thought of his own teacher, Socrates. One of the most famous sayings of Socrates that Plato remembered is that "the unexamined life is not worth living". Of course it is possible to drift through life, merely reacting to whatever presents itself moment by moment. But Socrates believed that what separates human beings from animals is our capacity to reflect and consider, to learn from the past and plan for the future. Only in this way, he thought, could a truly human happiness be achieved.

This view fits well with the approach of St Ignatius that we have been considering. One of the main ways to grow in happiness is to take time to examine my life on a regular basis. If I come to a realisation of why I have been created – and the answer to the question posed in the old Penny Catechism, "Why did God make me?", is a useful succinct summary here: "God made me to know him, to love him and to serve him in this world, and to be happy with him forever in the next" – then it makes sense to check out now and again whether I am in fact, in the different aspects of my life, loving and serving God.

Writing to the Christian community in Philippi, St Paul tells them, "I want you to be happy, always happy in the Lord; I repeat, what I want is your happiness." (*Ph* 4:4). This can be read as no more than a pious platitude, rolling off the tongue as easily as saying "Happy New Year", with no real thought. Surely it isn't possible to be always happy? Now it is certainly true that any human life is likely to have a mixture of happiness and unhappiness, with perhaps long stretches that seem more neutral. But this idea of the examined life puts happiness into a more central place. It is both the result of living the life for which we are created – there is a deep-rooted happiness that comes from loving and serving God, even if this leads me into difficult situations – and a kind of indicator that I am on the right track.

For Ignatius, this consolation, and its attendant happiness, become the chief criterion of discernment. I can review my past choices, and notice which of them led me into greater consolation. I can look to possible futures, and the choices that will lead to them, and try to come to a sense of which will be more likely to point me in the same way. On this road to happiness, examining my life for this consolation becomes the compass – or perhaps the sat-nav? – that points me in the right direction. (Incidentally there is in this model a counter-experience, desolation, which is the experience of feeling cut off from God, and finding the promptings of God distasteful. Noticing this in myself, and tracing it to its source, also has a role to play in discernment.)

5. Happiness as Personal

I felt my lungs inflate with the onrush of scenery – air, mountains, trees, people. I thought, "This is what it is to be happy".

Sylvia Plath, The Bell Jar

The next chapter (Chapter 6) will draw together the threads of this exploration of happiness as it has unfolded so far, suggesting some practical answers to the question of how to be happy. Before that, there is one further important point to be made. These pages have spoken, for the most part, in general terms. That is perhaps inevitable – they make up, after all, a booklet aimed at a general audience and not a personal letter addressed to you, an individual reader. But happiness is a deeply personal thing; when it comes down to specifics, no two people, no matter how similar they appear to be or closely they are united, are likely to be made happy by exactly the same things. So this chapter invites you to consider for yourself one question: what makes *you* happy?

What makes you happy?

If I pose this question to myself, I find that I spontaneously answer at different levels. There are things, objects, that make me happy. I'm writing this in early January, and my room has been brightened for these past weeks by a Christmas crib that a friend bought me, piece by piece, over several years. There are the things that I like to do on a day off – walking in the country, visiting historic buildings, taking time to be with family and friends. There are the longer-term sources of happiness: I like being a Jesuit, celebrating the sacraments and writing homilies and articles. And then there is the happiness of knowing myself loved and cared for by God, becoming more aware of this in prayer, and in trying to bring something of that loving care to others.

Clearly the last of those elements is common to anyone who tries to live a life shaped by religious faith. To know oneself loved, and to spread that love to others, is the ultimate source of happiness. But each of the other levels is much more individual. The objects that you surround yourself with will mean little to me – as we see in charity shops, filled with once treasured but now discarded possessions. The thought of spending an hour tracing the architectural development of an old church may well not be your idea of fun when you have a day to yourself. And your own longer-term sources of happiness – your family, the job that you do, the home that you have assembled – will be deeply affected by your own history and character.

There can be a temptation to think of these "lesser happinesses" as unimportant, at least for a person of faith, when compared with the happiness of knowing and serving God. But that would be to miss the truth of the incarnation, mentioned above in looking at mind, body and spirit. Since we are complex beings, happiness can reach us in different ways, and all are important. Indeed, they may often be linked. You experience a beautiful landscape, and there is the simple bodily pleasure of breathing clean air, appreciating the gleam of light on water, feeling the earth underfoot. This, perhaps, triggers what you might think of as a happiness of the mind – the landscape reminds you of a favourite holiday long ago, or a painting that has often spoken to you. And as you allow this happy experience to deepen, you find your spirits raised; on a given occasion, it may even point you towards God, in gratitude for the beauty in which you are immersed. Religion always runs the risk of detaching people from earthly cares and pleasures. Happiness, at all its levels, can have the benefit of rooting us firmly to the earth even as we aspire to heaven.

"Know thyself"

It is said that the entrance to the forecourt of the Temple of Apollo at Delphi had carved on its lintel the inscription "Know thyself". No doubt, if he had wanted to, God could have created a race of identical robots to know, love and serve him. It is clear, though, that this was not his intention. One of the main ways in which we differ from one another is in the particular mix of elements that serves to make each of us happy. Even identical twins will differ in this. So part of the answer to the question of how to be happy involves coming to this self-knowledge.

This sounds as if it should be a simple task, but often it is not. From an early age, children are taught about the kind of things that they ought, and ought not, to like. Some of this is clearly good and useful. There are pleasures associated with being able to read fluently that far outweigh the unhappiness that can be involved in having to work hard to master the alphabet. Playing with matches may seem like fun, but it is a pleasure to be discouraged in infants. But some of this early training can be hard to shake off. In later life, will I really be happier by spending an evening at a theatre attending a Shakespeare play, or sitting in front of the TV to catch up on my favourite soap?

Beyond that, there is the problem of what the Jesuit philosopher Gerard J Hughes calls "incompossibility". The lure of that soap, perhaps with a drink and some snacks, is a real one, and offers a prospect of real happiness this evening. Yet so is the desire to be fitter than I am, to go down to the gym for a punishing session on a treadmill. Maybe over time a balance can be struck between these two options, but with limited time on a given day both may not be possible, I may have to choose. Knowing which will contribute to my greater happiness, and being able to use that as the basis of my choice (and not simply be ruled by habit or immediate comfort) is not always easy.

The gym or the soap, the solo mountain hike or the meal with friends: I cannot know what will contribute most to your happiness (nor, indeed, you to mine). Fortunately, it is not important that I do. It is important that you yourself are aware of this, however, if you are to be able to live a life that does indeed make you happy, and in that way become a real blessing to those with whom you come into contact.

6. Practices Promoting Happiness

If you want others to be happy, practise compassion.
If you want to be happy, practise compassion.

Dalai Lama XIV, The Art of Happiness

The question of how to be happy can look as if it should have a simple answer. "Do this and this, and happiness is guaranteed." Some of the self-help books that take this question as their starting point promise exactly that. The secret of happiness is to be found in diet, or in meditation, in exercise, or in ditching toxic relationships. By contrast, the picture of happiness presented here is a more complex one. That is not to say that it is impossible to achieve, or is available only to spiritual high-flyers. But here are many factors to be taken into account in pursuing happiness, and many false trails that start off full of promise but ultimately lead nowhere.

This penultimate chapter attempts to draw together some of the threads of this discussion by presenting four things to do in order to be happy. As we have seen, the precise shape that these take will be different for different people. But they are, perhaps four essential practices for anyone who is serious about becoming a (more) happy person.

Focus elsewhere

Amateur astronomers, keen to see the dimmer stars and planets without the use of telescopes or other optical apparatus, are instructed not to look at them directly but to try and see them out of the corner of the eye. The reason for this has to do with the nature of the eyes' light receptor cells. Those dealing with colour vision, known as the cones, are grouped centrally, and are actually less acute than the monochrome receptors, the rods, which are more peripheral. So poor light is picked up better by the eye's edges. The comparison, though, is a good one for those looking for happiness. Stared at too intensely, it tends to disappear. Its presence can often be sensed more easily when your main gaze is brought to bear elsewhere.

Recall once again a time when you yourself were really happy. The chances are that it wasn't on a day when you set out saying to yourself "I'm going to do whatever it takes be happy today." You may well at that moment itself not even have stepped back from whatever you were doing at the time to reflect to yourself, "I'm really happy just now." Most likely it was only afterwards that you became aware of just how happy you were there and then. Or maybe, more usually, you experience a quiet background happiness in much of your life, a happiness that is there, and real, but which you only rarely remark upon.

It may well in fact be the case that the happiest people would not think it necessary to read books on finding happiness, or spend time considering how they themselves might grow in this quality. It is likely that they are kept busy with other things, and at times that are not thus filled are occupied in rest and relaxation, or in expressing the gratitude that they feel. Indeed, such people may express surprise that others think of them as distinctively happy; a certain lack of awareness may itself be a sign that a high level of happiness is being experienced.

In short, happiness is often best thought of as a by-product of other things – cultivating fulfilling relationships, or making an attitude of gratitude habitual in your life – rather than as a goal in itself to be focussed on too intently.

Monitoring

The idea of monitoring your happiness levels might seem to contradict the previous suggestion of focussing elsewhere. But it is perhaps the difference between pulling up a plant out of the ground obsessively to check whether the roots are growing as they should (a guarantee that they won't be), and checking now and again that the plant has all the light, water and fertiliser it needs to thrive and be healthy. Ideas expressed earlier about the value of the examined life suggested that discernment relies upon an awareness of happiness and consolation, thus the monitoring of these becomes an essential practice.

In the teaching of St Ignatius Loyola the chief place where this monitoring is carried out is in a prayer that he called the examen. His recommendation was that, on a daily basis, I turn to God and ask to be shown more clearly how God is currently present and active in my life. As that awareness deepens, I also ask to be shown how I have been responding to God's presence and action. At times no doubt my responses will have been poor, and I may resolve to repent and improve them in the future. But this is not meant to be primarily a prayer of repentance, an examination of conscience. Instead the main focus is on the good things that God is doing for me, is giving me. Ignatius believed that by doing this regular monitoring I would grow in gratitude for all of God's gifts, and by being more attuned to these, be more ready to respond in ways that make for my happiness.

Ignatian spirituality has at times been criticised as being overly individualistic, principally concerned with each single person in their relationship with God. One response to this is that Ignatius himself primarily thought of life as lived in community – our idea of the self-contained individual focussing solely on his or her own happiness would have been foreign to him. But it is also true that in recent years the notion of the examen has been expanded to look at relationships not simply with God and with my neighbour, but also with the whole of creation. How am I, and how are we, caring for the world around us, how responsibly are we exercising our God-given stewardship? Although there is not space to develop these considerations much more fully here, they are important ones for the quest for happiness. It is for instance clear that no individual is going to be in a condition to live a very happy life if climate change and ecological destruction are allowed to continue unchecked, wrecking the global environment. This point is developed at some length by Pope Francis in his 2015 encyclical, *Laudato Si'*. To give one example, he notes in paragraph 43: "Human beings too are creatures of this world, enjoying a right to life and happiness, and endowed with unique dignity. So we cannot fail to consider the effects on people's lives of environmental deterioration, current models of development and the throwaway culture."

Journaling is another practice that can serve the same end. In his poem *The Dry Salvages*, T.S. Eliot speaks of those who had "had the experience but missed the meaning". Often meaning and happiness are linked. If I am able to find meaning in my life, in the things that happen to me, it is easier to be happy even in times of difficulty. Writing a journal offers a chance to pause and to reflect, and thus to come to greater clarity about the meaning of my experiences. And, as with the examen, once I am clearer about what is going on there will often be more chance of doing what I can to build on what is good.

Service

When life is being regularly monitored in this way, another practice that seems from a Christian perspective to be productive of happiness is that of dedicating myself to the service to others. At first sight this is a surprising conclusion to reach. Certainly in the secular working world service is normally thought of as occupying a lowly place. Jobs involving a conspicuous element of service – those of shop assistants, waiters, nurses and care staff in homes for the elderly – are often among the poorest paid and least secure. They attract little of that public acclaim that is reserved for entrepreneurs, CEOs and captains of industry. This can be so even when it is realised how impossible society would be without their contribution.

The Christian scriptures come to a different conclusion. Towards the end of his public ministry, Jesus wants to give himself as fully as possible to those who have been closest to him. They celebrate one final meal together. In the gospels of Mark, Matthew and Luke this is marked by the breaking of bread and the blessing of wine, distributed to those present as Jesus says, "This is my body, this is my blood, given for you". John's gospel tells the story differently. For him, the central action of that evening came when Jesus washed the disciples' feet, normally the task of the lowest household servant. He then makes of them the same request that in the other gospels accompanies the eucharist – that they themselves should continue to do this in his memory. Here the request comes with a promise: if they will only behave in this way, they will be *makarioi*, a word that can be translated as blessed or happy.

When Paul writes to the Philippians that he wants them to be happy, he is speaking not merely of his own desires but of God's as well. This is easy to say, but difficult to remember, especially when life is at its most challenging. If the scriptures ask us to serve one another, it's not because this is difficult, or character-forming, or unpleasant but necessary, in the way that swallowing a foul-tasting medicine might be; it is because living lives of mutual service in this way is a sure road to happiness, even if it is one that can easily be overlooked.

Note, though, that it is not necessary to be a doormat to serve others in this way. Such service is not incompatible with standing up for yourself, having a strong sense of self-worth, and refusing to be pushed around. Jesus himself showed all these characteristics. Sometimes the best way to serve another person can be to refuse to co-operate with their unjust demands, and help them to see what would be better, for them and for other people, in a given situation. It is those individuals who are most confident in their own God-given gifts and talents who are often in the best position to serve, using those same gifts and talents for the benefit of others.

Sense of purpose

The picture of happiness being drawn here is one that is opposed to drift, of letting months, years and decades go by dictated solely by immediate whim or ingrained habit. A fourth practice that is conducive of promoting happiness, then, is the cultivation and maintenance of a sense of purpose. This is a viewpoint that isn't opposed to leisure, taking time off and simply relaxing. But leisure itself here finds its place within a purposeful framework.

If it is true, as Christians believe, that human beings are created to know, love and serve God, it is reasonable to suppose that doing this will make them happy, not just when fully united with God in heaven but also in the here and now. Screwdrivers can be used for all kinds of things: prising the lid off paint tins, acting as makeshift chisels, wedging doors open in the absence of a doorstop. But screwdrivers are designed with a single aim in mind, to tighten and loosen screws, and each part of them is intended to fulfil that aim. It is perhaps not fanciful to assume that a sentient screwdriver would be at its happiest tightening screws into joints, however it felt about being adapted to myriad other uses.

Awareness of a sense of purpose offers the objective pole of the monitoring that has been written about above. Subjectively, you look for the felt experience of consolation, of that kind of happiness that experience teaches comes from being attuned to God's will in the world. Objectively, you ask whether your actions accord with your stated sense of purpose. Is what you are doing in actual fact contributing to the knowledge, love and service of God? Taken together, these two reference points enable you to steer a course through life. If objectively you judge that you are living in accord with your sense of purpose, and subjectively experience consolation in doing so, you can be fairly sure that you are on the road to happiness. If the two judgements point in different directions (you judge that you're not serving God, but feel consoled; or are serving God, but experience ongoing desolation), a warning light is flashing. That becomes a sign for a deeper scrutiny of your manner of life, or your beliefs about God.

7. Happiness as Gift

Happiness, happiness, the greatest gift that I possess.
I thank the Lord that I've been blessed
with more than my share of happiness.

Bill Anderson

Happiness as gift, not achievement

The title of this booklet, *How to be Happy*, would fit in very nicely with many of the self-help books of a well-stocked bookstore. Some of what has been written here, for instance about not getting too caught up in material possessions, or the value of journaling, might also sit quite comfortably within those other pages. But there is a fundamental difference between self-help and the Christian outlook being explored here. Ultimately, for a follower of Jesus, happiness depends not on self-help but on God-help.

For when it comes down to it, the kind of happiness that a Christian is promised is not an achievement, a fitting reward for a good life well lived. It is rather a gift, a blessing from God which is freely given as an expression of God's graciousness. It cannot therefore be demanded, or guaranteed, or even earned, but must simply be received, with gratitude. It can however be expected, since it has been promised, and God is always faithful to his promises. But when and where it is experienced is ultimately not in the control of any individual.

The various tips, suggestions and practices put forward in these pages can do more than dispose a person to be on the look-out for the kind of places that this happiness is most likely to be found, and to recognise it and welcome it when it comes. This is not to say that the advice gathered here is either unnecessary or worthless. God has made us, as human beings, collaborators in our own salvation, and expects us to do what we can with the powers of reasoning and understanding that he has given us. It is indeed worthwhile to consider, as people have been doing for millennia, what makes for happiness and what gets in its way. This must never be done, though, in a way that makes it look like a slot-machine, that if I put the right actions or dispositions in at one end, God will guarantee immediate happiness as a result.

A conclusion such as this shouldn't be too surprising, since it is true of other areas of deep human experience. Think of love: there are things that I can do to make myself a more lovable person – accepting others as they are, showing an interest in them, not pushing my own needs ahead of theirs. But ultimately to be loved is a gift which it is not mine to command. It must of its nature be freely given, and my part is to recognise the gift and receive it with gratitude.

An afterword on heaven

Even for those who are most fortunate, the experience of happiness this side of the grave is likely to be intermittent, fluctuating, and unpredictable. We believe, though, that this will not always be the case. The true home of human happiness is in heaven, where we hope to be enabled to enjoy this gift with God uninterruptedly for eternity. Maybe a booklet on how to be happy should have started in heaven, and only gradually worked its way back down to earth?

One problem with that idea is that our knowledge of heaven is extremely limited. Even the great St Paul, when questioned about some of its details, becomes exasperated. "These are ridiculous questions!" he exclaims, when someone tries to pin him down on the mechanics of the resurrection. (*1 Co* 15:36). We do know that heaven is a state where all the conditions for happiness are met, and whatever might get in the way of our being happy has been removed. The precise nature of that heavenly happiness, how it will work, isn't known. Nor does it need to be for the present.

There is however perhaps one further clue to what heaven will be like, a clue that ties it in with what has been written earlier here. In the Apostles' Creed common to Christians, we profess belief in "the resurrection of the body". The book of Revelation, quoting the prophet Daniel, promises that there will be in the future "a new heaven and a new earth" (*Rv* 21:1). Our life in heaven will be no more ethereal than our life on earth here and now is. Human beings are, and will remain for all eternity, embodied spirits. This surely implies that there will be bodily happiness in heaven, as well as the joys of the mind and the spirit. Asking what these will be like risks the exasperation of St Paul. The resurrected body will be in some respects very different from the bodies that are at present so central to our way of being in the world, as can be seen in the case of the risen Christ, not immediately recognisable and able to pass through locked doors. But bearing these considerations in mind offers the assurance nevertheless of a truly human future beyond death.

What is clear is that ultimately the basis of heaven's happiness is to be united with God. Once we are joined with God in this way, there will be no more room for unhappiness or anything like it. Much of what has been written here has indeed been concerned with ways to become united more fully with God, and with God's will for the world, here and now. It is not surprising, then, that such a stance should make us most ready to receive happiness. Beyond that, we know that this happiness is what God wants for human beings, both eventually in heaven and even now, here on earth, to the extent that we are capable of receiving it. A Christian is one who should constantly live in the expectation of being happy, and of doing everything possible to recognise and receive that gift of happiness when it is offered.